Editors' Note

In *Medjugorje: A New Portfolio of Images*, the editors have attempted to bring together new photos and more information regarding the extraordinary and unusual occurrences which have been transpiring in a little, out-of-the-way corner of the world over the past several years where the Blessed Virgin Mary is said to have been appearing on an almost daily basis to a handful of Yugoslavian teenagers.

While awaiting the judgment of the competent ecclesiastical authorities, the publishers, out of a sense of duty to inform, want to participate in the diffusion of news regarding these well-known experiences, and they have chosen to do so by means of this collection of several excerpts from the many messages which the Madonna has given through these youngsters from Medjugorje to the people of the world in this, the last decade of the twentieth century.

The subject treated here, and the impressions left by the photographs themselves, cannot leave indifferent the reader who — certainly free to express himself or herself in favor of or against these apparitions — might feel encouraged to go to Medjugorje to strengthen or disprove the testimony of many who, as pilgrims to that place, have returned with their own faith re-found or reinforced.

Emanuele - Mir

MEDJUGORJE

A New Portfolio of Images

ALBA · HOUSE   NEW · YORK

SOCIETY OF ST. PAUL, 2187 VICTORY BLVD., STATEN ISLAND, NEW YORK 10314

The original edition of this book was published in 1985 by
Bertoncello Artigrafiche, Cittadella (Padova), Italy under
the title: *Un evento per immagini — Medjugorje*.

This second English language version follows the
German expanded edition: *Ein Ereignis in Bildern —
Medjugorje*, published by Miriam-Verlag, Jestetten.
Translated by Ivanka C.R. Roberts

Printed in August, 1990, from type set in the U.S.A.
ISBN: 0-8189-0585-9

A special thanks is extended to the following who freely collaborated in this collection of photographs and
messages: G. Amorth, A. Baron, F. Bellini, A. Bonifacio, A. Frassinelli, A. Gava, U. Manenti, A. Muti,
M. Paccagnan, F. Paravicini, R. Paravel, T. Pasquazzo, M. Rastrelli, M. Valenta, and F. Vatta. A number of
the new photos were supplied by the Medjugorje Prayer Movement of Vienna. I. Bottino and B. Rind were
the authors of the German text.

*This collection is dedicated
to all generous young people
to whom the Virgin Mary
has confidently entrusted
the future of the human race.*

Printed in Italy

Bertoncello Artigrafiche, Cittadella (Padova)

Table of Contents

Introduction

News of the apparitions of the Madonna in Yugoslavia has spread throughout the world. Since July 24, 1981, the Blessed Virgin Mary — who calls herself the "Queen of Peace" — is said to have been appearing in Medjugorje, a small village in the province of Bosnia-Herzegovina in Yugoslavia. She has come on an almost daily basis to a group of young people between the ages of 18 and 23 (when the apparitions began they were between 10 and 15 years old). The frequency of the visits initially made the unusual occurrence seem almost totally unbelievable. However, there is now much evidence to support the claim and many — though admittedly not all — who have investigated the events during the past decade have testified to their authenticity.

Through the visionaries, Mary has proclaimed a message of peace and reconciliation to the world: *I would like to be with you, to convert you and to reconcile the whole world.* But she also states quite clearly that peace requires that people return to God. It is dependent on conversion, prayer, fasting and the more frequent reception of the sacraments. In her maternal love, she does not hesitate to urge us strongly to *take the messages seriously, because God is not joking with mankind.*

Over time these messages have attained greater spiritual intensity, particularly through the many prayer groups that have been founded at the request of the Madonna. By means of these visions, Mary has guided the community of Medjugorje through a life of intense daily and nightly devotions, of sacrifice and fasting, of charity and hospitality towards others, of participation in the Eucharist, confession and the recitation of the Rosary. The inhabitants of the place have accepted the messages with extraordinary good will and live their lives in accord with them, thus providing communal testimony, by their genuinely Christian way of living, to their authenticity to an extent unprecedented in the history of other visions. We must also bear in mind that we are dealing with people from families which, despite four hundred years of Turkish rule, have kept their faith intact, an act often associated with heroic sacrifices; people who still call themselves "Roman Catholics, faithful to the Pope and to the Apostolic Church," who were, until recently, dominated by a harsh and godless communist regime.

Why have these apparitions been occurring over the past ten years or so? Only because the Father has permitted it.

Mary says: *Thank God, the Father, for having allowed me the possibility of remaining in your midst for so long. Through your prayers and fasting, help me to assure that the plan of salvation which my Son, Jesus, has prepared for you and the whole world, can be realized. — Pray that you may be open to all that God wishes to accomplish through you; thank God by the way in which you live, and take delight in everything that He is able to accomplish through each of you for the good of all mankind.*

"Peace! Peace! Peace!"

My peace be with you! says the Risen Lord. (Jn 20:19)

And so does the Madonna in Medjugorje, who never tires of repeating the message: *My dear children, I summon you to peace. Live with peace in your hearts and in your surroundings so that everyone will know that this peace comes not from you, but from God. . . . Rejoice with me! Celebrate the birth of Jesus with my peace, the peace with which I, as your mother, as the Queen of Peace, have come to you. I give you my special blessing: proclaim it to everyone you meet, so that everyone can have this peace within* (December 25, 1988).

The rocky peak of Križevac.

Her call for peace is not without reason. She repeats it every day with the patience of a mother who, seeing the world full of *such tensions*, clearly admonishes it: *If the world keeps on going in this way, it will quickly find itself on the brink of ruin. It will find salvation only in peace. And it will only have peace if it finds God. I have come to tell everyone that God exists, and that life and peace can only be found in Him. . . . In God there are no divisions. . . . Jesus is the sole Mediator. Therefore, I say to you: Be converted and reconciled to Him. Pray, fast, practice charity. The only way to attain peace for oneself and peace with others is to pray* (October 29, 1983).

The messages which I have transmitted on the part of my Son are for everybody, but in a special way for the Holy Father, and through him for all the world. . . .

From Medjugorje I want to say to the Holy Father: The word which I have come to announce is PEACE! It is my desire that he transmit this message to all the world . . . that he be courageous in announcing peace and love to all the world. . . . May he not feel himself to be the father of Catholics only, but of all peoples. . . .

My message to him is that he strive to reunite all Christians with his preaching and that he transmit to young people that which God inspires him to say in his prayers (to Jelena, September 16, 1983).

As a good mother, Mary affirms her children to whom she offers the tender yet firm advice which she once gave at Cana: *Do whatever He tells you!* (Jn 2:5)

The Madonna awaits her children with a welcoming gesture. In the background is the church of St. James in Medjugorje.

9

"Peace must reign between God and the individual and all peop

Peace! Peace! Peace! This is the dominant and most insistent message of Mary to the visionaries anxious to know her name: *I am the Queen of Peace!*

It is the message to which the Blessed Virgin Mary called the greatest attention and which heaven itself confirmed on the night of June 25, 1981, when the extraordinary, luminous sign with the word MIR (Peace) appeared written in large letters across the sky between Mount Križevac and Mount Podbrdo, clearly visible to the pastor and the inhabitants of the whole valley.

Peace, peace! But there is no peace! (Jr 6:14)

The rocky peak of Podbrdo, where the first apparitions took place. It was here that the Madonna revealed herself as the "Queen of Peace."

"Pray! Pray! Pray!"

Mary, the first and most faithful of the disciples of the Lord, at Medjugorje does no more than draw the attention of the world to the Gospel of Jesus and to the Jesus of the Gospel: *In those days Jesus went by himself alone to a mountain where he spent the night in prayer* (Lk 6:12).

She says: *You have forgotten that with prayer and fasting you keep war at bay and even suspend the laws of nature. So start to pray. Your faith is weak because you pray so little. Without constant prayer, you cannot sense the greatness and beauty of the grace that God offers you. Therefore, dear children, you should fill your hearts at all time with prayers, however small they are. I am with you and watch unceasingly over every heart entrusted to my care* (January 26, 1989).

Like a wise teacher, she suggests that they start little by little, with a minimum of seven Our Fathers, Hail Marys, Glory Be to Gods and the Creed; with a fast of bread and water on Fridays because, without *prayer and fasting*, conversion is difficult, and without conversion one cannot live in communion with God and one's brothers and sisters.

My dear children, again I ask you to pray with your hearts, because if you pray with your hearts, the ice in your brothers' hearts will melt and all obstacles will be removed. For all who desire to be converted, this will be easy, because conversion is a gift that you must request for your fellow man from God (January 23, 1986).

The visionaries in ecstasy during an apparition. From left to right: Vicka, Jakov, Ivanka, Mirjana, Marija and Ivan.

The conversion proposed by the Blessed Virgin — with the purpose of realizing the command of Jesus, *Love your enemies . . . pray for those who mistreat you* (Lk 6:27-28) — is the fruit of grace and of a superabundant effusion of the love of God in one's heart.

For that reason, it is necessary that we plead with incessant, confident prayer, that the Sacred Heart of Jesus might pour forth upon us this grace and love, and that through His mediation it might bear abundant fruit in us.

Mary reassures us in this regard: *In your prayer, I ask you to turn to Jesus. I am your Mother, and I will intercede with Him on your behalf.* Who, in fact, knows better than she the fidelity of her Son to these, His own words: *If you, wicked as you are, know how to give good things to your children, how much more will your Father in heaven give the Holy Spirit (that is, the gift of Love) to those who ask Him for it?* (Lk 11:13)

Therefore, her messages constantly draw our attention to prayer: *Pray, my children! I repeat again: Pray! You must come to know that prayer is the most important thing in your lives* (January 3, 1984).

I realize that I talk about prayer very often. But you should know that there are many people in the world who do not pray, who do not even know what they should say in prayer (to Jelena, January 15, 1984).

13

Mary always keeps her appointments

The moment Mary appears to the visionaries, they make the sign of the cross and all of them fall to their knees simultaneously.

A group of the faithful gathered in the parish church of St. James.

"Pray together in the family"

I would be very happy if families would begin to pray together for a half hour in the morning and in the evening. . . . This evening I would like to ask you to pray that the Holy Spirit descend on your families and your parish during this novena (the novena to Pentecost). God wishes to bestow gifts upon you with which you will glorify Him (June 2, 1984).

Don't look to hear extraordinary voices; take up the Gospels and read them. . . . There everything is clear. . . . Prayer must be given first place. . . . With the five Our Fathers, Hail Marys, Glory Be to Gods and the Creed, unite your prayer to that of the Holy Spirit. And if it is possible, it would be good for you to recite at least a third of the Rosary. . . . When you pray at home in the evenings, pray for the conversion of sinners, because the world finds itself in great sin. . . . I ask you to pray the Rosary every night with your families (September 27, 1984).

The work in the fields has ended; now devote yourselves to prayer! Prayer should take first place within your families (November 1, 1984).

Dear children, today I invite you to renew the prayer life of your families; encourage the other children to pray and the toddlers to go to Mass (March 7, 1985).

Dear children, I would like all families to devote themselves to the Sacred Heart every day. I would be very happy if every family were to unite in prayer (October 20, 1983).

Pray, my children! I keep repeating that you should pray since prayer is irreplaceable in your life (to Jelena, January 1, 1984).

My dear children, you know that the Day of Joy is drawing closer, but you will achieve nothing without love. Therefore, first of all begin to love your own families and everyone in the parish. Then you will be able to receive and love all those who come here. This week should be a week in which you learn to love (December 13, 1984).

Dear children, during the next and following days people from all nations will be coming to this parish. Therefore I call on you to love. Above all, love the members of your families! Then you will be capable of receiving and loving everyone who comes here (June 6, 1985).

I am pleased with all of you who are on the path to holiness and, through your testimony, I ask you to help all those who do not know how one lives in holiness. Your families should be the place where holiness is born. Help everyone to live in a devout way, particularly the members of your own families (July 24, 1986).

My children, I invite you to live the messages I give you every day — especially since I want to guide you closer to the Sacred Heart of Jesus. Therefore, today I invite you to devote yourselves to my dear Son, so that each of your hearts will belong to Him. I also invite you to devote yourselves to my Immaculate Heart. I would like you to devote yourselves individually, as a family, and as a parish, so that everything will belong to God through me.

My dear children, pray so that you will understand the importance of the message that I give you. I ask nothing for myself, but everything to save your souls. Satan is strong; therefore, dear children, bind yourselves to my maternal heart through steadfast prayer (October 25, 1988).

I am your good Mother and Jesus is your best friend. . . . Don't be afraid, but give Him your heart and tell Him about all your sufferings. Thus you will be revitalized through prayer. Your hearts will be set free and you will be at peace.

Following Mary's appeal, a family gathers for prayer at 6:00 in the morning.

Meetings with two bishops

A miraculous event which drew a lot of attention was the instantaneous healing of Diana Basile. Born in 1940, married and the mother of three, Diana has been afflicted since 1972 with multiple sclerosis aggravated by several diverse problems: a serious difficulty in walking, the nearly complete immobility of her right arm, urinary incontinence, etc. On May 23, 1984, she made a pilgrimage to Medjugorje.

"I found myself on the sidewalk just outside the church. A lady from Bologna helped me up the steps. I had no desire to enter the chapel of the apparitions since someone had told me that only priests were allowed in. But a French priest told me to stay and, as soon as the door was opened, he invited me to enter. I remained in the chapel for the duration of the apparition. I can hardly remember what happened though I was astonished at the way in which the visionaries fell to their knees at the same time when the Madonna appeared. My life passed before my eyes, almost like a film. Once the apparition was over, without being aware of what I was doing, I followed the visionaries who returned to the main church to join the people in prayer. Only then did I realize that I was completely cured."

Mrs. Diana Basile recounts the story of her healing to Bishop Pavao Zanić, Bishop of Mostar who has publicly expressed his misgivings about the events occurring in Medjugorje.

In 1981, Bishop Franić came to Medjugorje incognito and, like every other pilgrim, took part in the evening liturgy. On December 16, 1988, on the eve of his official retirement from the archdiocese, he came to Medjugorje again, this time to celebrate the twelve o'clock Mass in the chapel of the apparitions together with the Franciscans of Herzegovina. He thanked the Madonna for all the mercies that he had received during the thirty-eight years of his episcopate, and entrusted the rest of his days to her Immaculate Heart, praying that he spend these in true faith and spiritual joy. He gave his thoughts about the charges of fraud leveled against the priests of the parish from some ecclesiastical quarters: "I did not come across any rebellious priests, but rather men who were humble and courageous members of their order, strong in faith."

He confirmed his own personal certainty about the presence of Mary in Medjugorje and about the effect of her call to love. He is convinced that Medjugorje has won more people to the faith than all the lay missions that have been operated at great expense since the end of the war. In fact, on April 17, 1985, he declared to the Yugoslavian Bishops Conference: "If several thousand persons from Split and its surroundings are persevering in prayer, Medjugorje must be thanked. I have studied the facts; I went back to the place in order to be able to tell my faithful whether or not I approved of their making a pilgrimage to Medjugorje. I assisted at Mass, I spoke with the visionaries, I saw the pilgrims. As far as prayer, fasting and conversion are concerned, Medjugorje is bearing fruit which is abundant and evident. . . . For my part, I consider that we are dealing here with events that are supernatural."

Bishop Franić, former Archbishop of Split and Makarska and Past President of the Yugoslavian Bishops Commission on Doctrine and Faith, seen here with the visionaries Ivan and Marija, shortly before an apparition.

"Fast and be converted!"

During those forty days in the desert, Jesus had nothing to eat (Lk 4:4).

One of Mary's most urgent recommendations is to fast. More than that, she has made fasting a condition for obtaining the impossible from God.

Pray and fast every Friday on bread and water . . . Give up those television programs which are harmful to the family because after watching such programs you will be distracted and unable to pray . . . (December 8, 1981).

No one is dispensed from fasting, except those who are gravely ill. Prayer and works of charity cannot take its place. Those who cannot fast, however, are free to substitute fasting with prayer, works of charity and confession (July 21, 1982).

If it is not possible for all to fast on the same days, each should fast when he or she can (to Jelena, November 16, 1983).

It is not fasting if you eat fish instead of meat; that is abstinence. A true fast entails the renunciation of all sin, but it is also necessary for the body to take part in this renunciation (December 30, 1983).

On Thursdays — the day consecrated to the Eucharist — each one should find a way of giving up something: the one who smokes should give up smoking; the one who likes an alcoholic drink should give it up; each one should give up something that is pleasurable.

Ivan, shown here with a friend, is faithful to his fast on bread and water.

20

Reforming our life, which the Blessed Virgin keeps emphasizing, requires us to fulfill the Lord's command: *Love your enemies; do good to those who hate you. Bless those who curse you and pray for those who mistreat you* (Lk 6:27-28).

Let everyone know as soon as possible that I desire their conversion.

Give me your hearts! I want to change them completely. I want to remake them. I want them to be pure. You know that I love you and will protect you.

Dear children, I would like you to become my prophets, children who bring peace, love and conversion to their fellow men.

Such conversion is the fruit of God's grace and infinite love which He liberally bestows on those who ask Him for it. Prayer, therefore, is indispensable.

My dear children, without prayer there is no peace. For this reason I tell you to pray for peace. Pray before the crucifix.

Even those crosses of your own making are in the plan of God. . . .

Climb the mountain and pray before the cross that has been set up there. You know that it represents the sacrifice of Jesus.

Place all your problems and troubles in my hand. Live by my messages. Pray! Pray! Pray!
(January 2, 1989).

Every month in Medjugorje, during the three days which precede the first Sunday of the month, the parishioners carefully prepare themselves for their monthly confession.

A pilgrimage without end

My dear children, reform your lives! You in the parish, take my invitation to heart. . . . Thus those who come here will likewise be converted.

I know that you pray for long periods, but try really hard. Pray even during the evening after you have finished your day. Seat yourselves in your room and say to Jesus: "Thank you!" If at night you fall asleep praying, you will awaken in the morning thinking of Jesus and you will be able to pray to Him for peace.

But if you fall asleep with a million distractions, you will awaken the next morning feeling oppressed and you may even forget to pray. . . . Be patient; be constant!

The spirit of the world is a sinful spirit. . . . It seems to you that it is not sinful because

Scene of the church around which some pilgrims are gathered during the celebration of the Eucharist.

you live in an atmosphere of peace. . . .
How many, though, there are whose faith is
half-hearted and who do not listen to Jesus!

If you only knew how much I suffer, you
would never sin again. I need all of your
prayers. Pray!

**Croatian women climb the hill of the
apparitions barefooted and praying.**

It is interesting to note with what emphasis the Madonna summons her children to purify and cleanse themselves through the Sacrament of Reconciliation: *If Christians were to start confessing once a month, whole regions would soon begin to be spiritually restored.*

Do not confess simply out of habit and then afterwards remain unchanged. That is wrong! Confession should strengthen your faith. It should be an incentive to you, and it should bring you closer to Jesus. If confession means nothing to you, it is truly unlikely that you will ever be converted (November 7, 1983).

It is necessary to call upon people to confess once a month, particularly on the first Saturday of the month. Up till now, I have said very little about this. I have merely requested people to go to confession more often. Soon I will be giving you several practical messages that are important for our times. Be patient, for the time is not yet right. Do what I have told you. There are many who do not obey. The monthly confession will act as a medicine for the Western Church. This message must be proclaimed to all the world (August 6, 1982).

Since the confessionals inside the church are never sufficient, priests make do on chairs set up outdoors.

The only water fountain available, in the early years of the visions, to quench the thirst of the pilgrims.

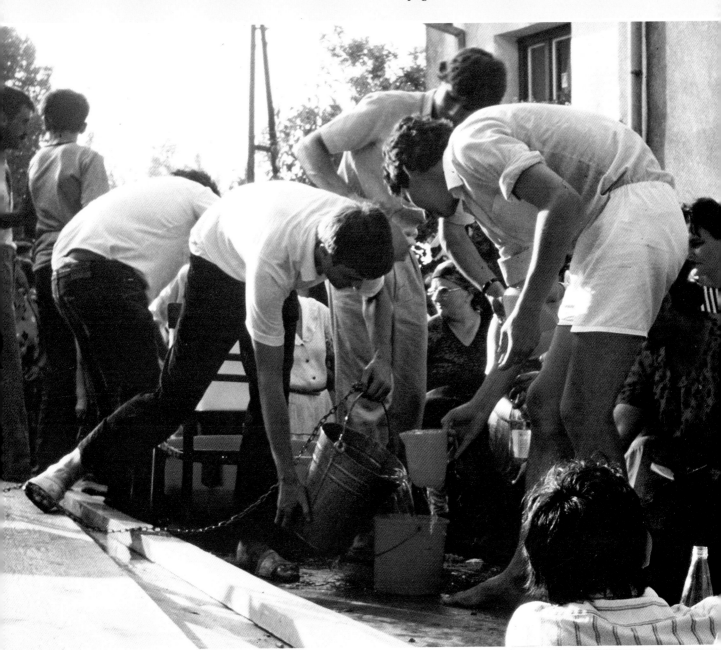

"You shall be the sign . . ."

My dear children! Today I invite you to enter into combat with Satan in a special way by means of prayer. Satan will fight even harder against you now that you are wise to his activities! Arm yourselves against him and overcome him with the Rosary in your hand (August 8, 1985).

You know that I love you and that, because of my love for you, I am here to show you the way to peace and salvation for your souls. I would like you to listen to me. Do not allow Satan to lead you astray. Satan is relatively strong and, therefore, I want you to offer your prayers to me for those who are under his influence, so that they can be saved. Give testimony through your lives and sacrifice yourselves for the salvation of the world. I am with you and I thank you. In heaven you shall receive the reward that your Father has promised you. Therefore, my dear children, do not be afraid! If you pray, Satan cannot harm you because you are God's children and He is watching over you! Pray! Always keep your Rosary close at hand as a sign to Satan that you belong to me (February 25, 1988).

Here is a description of that last apparition to Ivanka:

May 6: The Madonna appeared for about two minutes to Vicka, Jakov, Marija and Ivanka, but she continued the dialogue with Ivanka alone for another six minutes. In these eight minutes all together, the Madonna revealed the 10th secret and finished telling her about the future of the world. She then told her that she would wait for her alone at home on the following day.

May 7: Ivanka had the apparition at home. This is how she described it to Father Slavko: "As usual, just as she had on all the other days, my Mother greeted me with these words, *May Jesus Christ be praised!* and I answered her, 'May He be praised forever.' She stayed with me for an hour. Never had I seen her so lovely. She was so gentle and beautiful. . . . She had the most wonderful gown which shone like silver and gold. With her were two angels dressed in the same kind of gown. I cannot find words adequate to describe such beauty. Moments like that have to be lived.

"She asked me what I most desired at that moment. I answered her, 'to see my earthly mother' who had died a month before the apparitions of 1981. She smiled at me and then my mother appeared. I saw her. She was radiant. The Madonna told me to get up. My mother then embraced and kissed me saying: 'My daughter, I'm so proud of you!' She kissed me again and disappeared. The Madonna then continued: *My darling daughter, this will be our last meeting. Don't be sad, because I shall return every year on the anniversary of these apparitions.*

"*Don't think that you've done something wrong, and that this is why I am not coming any more. You embraced the plans that my Son and I had for you with your whole heart. The graces which you and your companions have received have never been given to anyone on earth! You must be happy. I am your Mother, and I love you with all my heart, Ivanka. I thank you for responding to my invitation and to that of my Son and for always patiently standing by Him, and for continuing to do so as long as He desires. My child, you must tell your friends that my Son and I will always be with you whenever you need us.*"

Ivanka asked the Madonna for permission to kiss her and her request was granted. Then Mary blessed her, saying with a smile: *Go in God's peace.* She slowly disappeared, and the two angels disappeared with her.

In the years since the last apparition, Mary has kept her promise to meet her every year on June 24, the day of the first apparition.

Ivanka is now married and the mother of a beautiful daughter whom she has named Christina.

Ivanka Ivanković, who was half-orphaned upon the death of her mother, was born in Bijakovići on June 21, 1966. She was the first to see the Madonna on June 24, 1981. For her, the apparitions ceased on May 7, 1985.

"Satan's power will be destroyed"

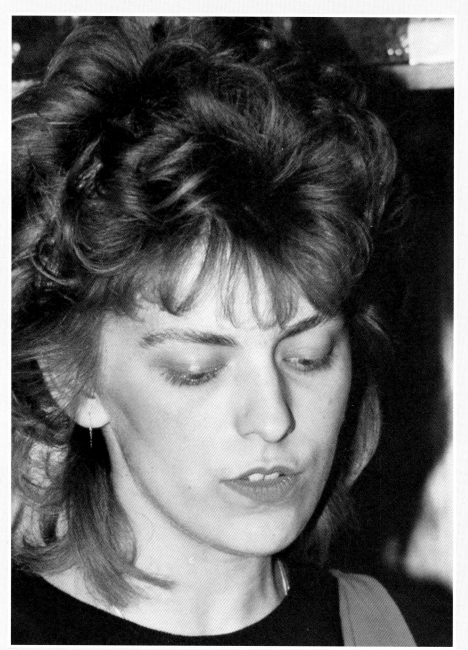

The Virgin did not spare this visionary from meeting the Prince of Darkness in one of her visions. But she immediately explained why:

It was necessary for you to realize that Satan exists. He has God's permission to test the Church, but not to destroy it. When the secrets which I am entrusting to you come to pass, the power of Satan will be broken. For the present, he has become aggressive. He destroys marriages, sets priests against one another, is responsible for many individuals' obsessions. . . . Therefore protect yourself from him through prayer and fasting and above all through community prayer. Carry signs of your faith with you (medallions, crosses, etc.) *and keep them in your homes; renew your use of holy water. Satan cannot do anything to those whose faith in God is strong* (To Mirjana).

Mirjana Dragičević in prayer. She is from Bijakovići, but lived with her family in Sarajevo. The tenth secret was revealed to her on December 25, 1982. Since then she has had no further daily visions. Mirjana was married in 1989.

The Blessed Virgin now only appears to Mirjana on her birthday or on special occasions such as, for instance, on March 19, 1984, to clarify some details relative to the ten secrets confided to her. These have been written down on a piece of paper which, at a time that will be indicated by the Blessed Virgin, will be able to be read, by a special grace, only by Father Petar Ljubičić, chosen by Mirjana for the revelation of the secrets.

It is a piece of paper whose contents, which deal with the present situation of the world, cause great sorrow to the Blessed Mother and bring tears to her eyes at the thought of her *non-believing children and those who listen to her but do not reform their lives* as well as of *those who live only to make money*. They also cause Mirjana to weep with intense sorrow when she sees people doing what they shouldn't do.

For all of these, her children, the Virgin invites Mirjana to pray without tiring. She did so on the occasion of the last apparition in which Mary took the Rosary of the young girl and said to her, *The Rosary is not an ornament. It must be prayed.*

There are many serious reasons to pray in spite of all obstacles. One of the things about which the Virgin steadfastly insists is the cultivation of loving relationships with our brothers and sisters of other religions, the elimination of rivalries and the removal of the walls that keep us apart. Mary repeatedly states that all are her children — Moslems, Orthodox and Catholics alike — because Jesus is the sole Mediator for all. Only He can bring salvation to everyone. She is extremely distressed that so many of her children, irrespective of the religion they adhere to, live as if God did not exist. Unfortunately, there is still a great lack of faith in the world. The times themselves speak to us of the urgency to pray for peace and to reform our lives, but few are being converted.

On October 25, 1985, the Blessed Virgin appeared to Mirjana as she had on several occasions during the preceding months. During the seven-minute apparition, she showed her the first warning. Mirjana wept and asked, "But will this happen so quickly?" Then she added: "How can God be so hard-hearted?" Mary replied: *It will all come to pass but God is not hard-hearted. Look around you and see what people are doing, and you will no longer say that God is hard-hearted. But you mustn't be afraid, because I am here.*

Father Petar Ljubičić was present, and Mirjana will tell him about the first warning three days before it comes to pass.

"Mass should be the focal point of your day!"

My children, I would like the Holy Mass to become the gift of the day for you. Look forward to it expectantly. Count the hours till it begins, because Jesus gives Himself to you in the Holy Mass. Pray often that the Holy Spirit might renew your parish. If people attend Mass only half-heartedly, they will go home empty and with cold hearts (to Jelena, March 30, 1984).

Not only are the crowds of faithful enormous, but the priest concelebrants are also many as these photos of a Mass in progress and the distribution of Holy Communion clearly show.

My dear children, God would like to make you devout. Therefore, He invites you to total devotion through me. The Holy Mass is to be your life. You must understand the church is the house of God, the place where you find cleansing, and the place where you will be shown the path to God. Come and pray! Reverence is due to every consecrated church because that is where God-made-man dwells night and day (April 25, 1988).

Prayer is a colloquy with God. . . . It enables you to understand God. . . . It makes it possible for you to enter into the fullness of joy. Prayer is life!

The night between the 24th and the 25th of June, 1985, the Madonna invited the visionaries to the top of Mt. Križevac for an extraordinary apparition. To Ivan she said: *I am happy above all at the large number of young people who are present.*

My dear children, this cross was also part of God's plan when it was erected. At this time, especially, you should go to the mountain and pray before the cross. I need your prayers (August 10, 1984).

My children, I stand by the cross almost every day. My Son bore the cross. He suffered on the cross. And through the cross He brought salvation to the world. Every day I ask my Son to forgive the sins of the world (December 31, 1981).

As you joyfully worship before the cross at this time, it is my hope that the crosses of your own making will also be joyfully embraced by you. Pray above all for the grace to accept sickness and suffering with love, as Jesus accepted the cross. Only if you do will I be able to bestow on you the mercies and healing that Jesus permits me to (September 11, 1986).

My children, make the cross the center of your attention. Pray before the cross because great mercies come from it. Devote yourselves to the cross in your homes. Promise that you will never offend Jesus or the cross, nor mock them through any kind of blasphemy (September 12, 1985).

The rock strewn path that leads to the summit of Mt. Križevac.

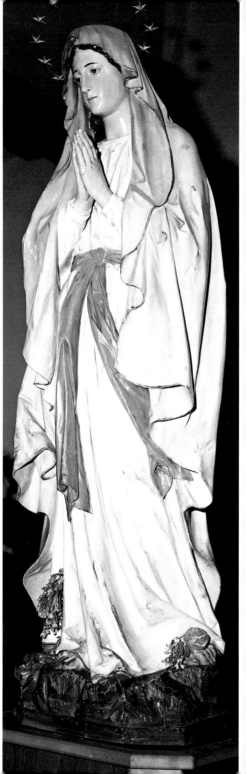

My children! I thank you for all the love you have given me. You know that my love for you is boundless. Every day I ask the Lord to help you feel the love that I have for you!

My dear children, tonight your mother would like to invite you to pray for all the young people throughout the world. Pray, too, for their parents so that they will know how to raise their children in such a way that their faith can grow, and that they can guide their children along the right path in life. Pray, dear children, because young people today find themselves in a very difficult situation. Help them, and assist those parents who give their children the wrong advice (October 24, 1988).

I am with you and I thank you. In heaven you shall receive the reward your Father has promised you. Therefore, my dear children, do not be afraid! (February 25, 1988).

The statue of the Immaculate Virgin Mary was placed once again in the center of the church in April of 1985.

Mary has a special, very personal plan for each visionary; each has a specific mission to perform for the good of mankind.

"At the beginning, my parents would not let me climb the hill of the apparitions. Even so, I saw the Madonna at the same time that she was appearing to my friends."

My dear children, this evening your mother rejoices with you and is happy. I would like to give you love, because you are to take this love to all people. You are to give it to them all. I would like to give you all peace, so that you can take this peace to all people. And above all, you should bring this peace to your own families, particularly where there may be some ill feeling. My dear children, I would like you to renew the prayer life of your families and invite others to do the same. Your mother will help you (October 17, 1988).

Ivan Dragičević, born on May 25, 1965, also comes from Bijakovići. He has overcome his initial shyness and given ample proof of his deep sense of responsibility. Now that he has ended his military service, he is totally at Mary's disposal, above all for the nighttime meetings on Križevac.

When he was ill, the Blessed Virgin gave him this message: *Dear son! Dedicate all the prayers you recite at home each night for the conversion of sinners because the world is immersed in serious evils. Recite the Rosary every evening.*

My dear children, this evening your mother would like to invite you to pray with your hearts. This prayer is very necessary for all people at this time. Do not merely pray with your lips; do not pray without knowing what you are saying. At this time, I need your prayers because there are many things that I would like to see accomplished. I would like you to work with me on these. . . . I need you. Therefore, pray. Pray with your hearts (October 31, 1988).

My dear children, I would like you to become my prophets, to become my children who prophesy peace, love and conversion. I would like you to become a sign to others (January 2, 1989).

Jakov Colo, the youngest of the visionaries, has lost both of his parents. He was born in Bijakovici on March 6, 1971. Notwithstanding his young age, he has shown a surprising degree of spiritual maturity.

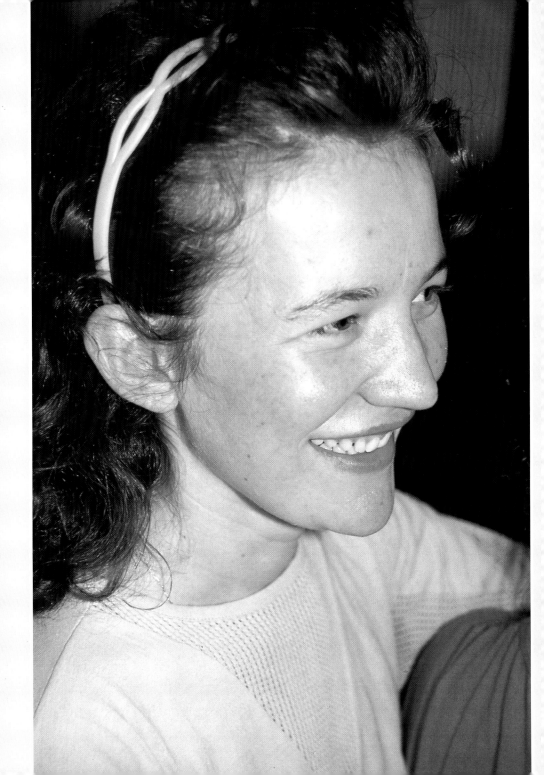

I came to you because I found faith here. I chose your parish and I intend to watch over it. I will care for it with love for I desire that all of you be mine. I wish that those who are with me and with my Son were more numerous. . . .

Tell those who do not see me that they should believe as if they did. . . .

As your Mother, I love each one of you at every moment. If you are in trouble, do not be afraid because I love you even then, even when you are far from me and from my Son.

Please, I beg you! Don't let my heart weep tears of blood for the loss of souls caused by sin. Therefore, have faith, fast and pray!

Vicka Ivanković, born in Bijakovići on September 3, 1964, is the oldest of the visionaries and the most outgoing of them all. She most willingly lends herself to answering people's questions. Her mother says of her: "The more I see my daughter suffer, the happier she seems. I don't understand it."

36

Pray! Pray! Pray! Through you people will believe when they see your faith. If you want to be strong in the face of evil, develop a lively conscience. I repeat: Pray, especially every morning. Read a passage from the Gospel. Plant the seed of God's word within you and let it come alive within you often during the day, especially during moments of discouragement, and in the evening you will be stronger.

If you want to be truly happy, lead a simple, humble life. Pray a lot and don't try to delve too deeply into problems. Let God resolve them for you.

Marija Pavlović, born on April 1, 1965, is the one among the visionaries who, even before the apparitions, was the most faithful to prayer. Her habitual reserve often reminds people of the figure of St. Bernadette of Lourdes. Recently, in order to save her brother from certain death, she donated one of her kidneys and is still in the process of recuperating.

37

"You shall bear witness to me!"

Father Jozo Zovko is one of the most trustworthy witnesses to the presence of the Blessed Virgin Mary in Medjugorje because his path, blessed by the Virgin, led from stubborn disbelief to the most unshakable faith in the visions, which his 21-month imprisonment has strengthened even further and imbued with prophetic light.

From his own report:
"One could say that I was the only one who didn't believe. I couldn't. . . . I kept thinking: What if these atheists are manipulating the visionaries because they want to discredit our work and our Church? . . . I openly stated that I did not believe. I was afraid of coming into conflict with heaven, but I didn't want the people in my parish, in my church, saying that we needed to believe in something like that (the apparitions of the Blessed Virgin). Then, during the prayer of the gathered community the Madonna appeared. She was standing twenty feet or so from the choir, in the middle of the church. She appeared and said in front of everyone: *Recite the Rosary every day; pray together.*

"She used exactly the same words as in the message that Jakov had brought to everyone present two hours earlier. The Madonna had not done this because of Jakov. The Mother of God had done it because of me; she wanted me to believe! The Madonna wants us all to believe. The Madonna wants you to believe, too.

"Believing in the Madonna and her messages means obeying her requests and living according to them. The Madonna referred us to the Rosary. Why? Because our Rosary signifies life; it means remembering the usual and unusual events in Jesus' life, things that have not all been written down . . . because Jesus lives in us . . . and through our lives we compose the life of Jesus and add to it.

"The Madonna wants the Rosary to become a part of our church and our families again. The Rosary is the daily prayer of the family, the prayer that nourishes us, that allows us to encounter God and that is a blessing to us.

"*Pray together* means that you should pray with your wife, your children, your parents in your home. . . ."

Father Jozo Zovko, who was transferred to Tihaljina, has never tired of spreading the messages of the Queen of Peace with the force of his testimony and the clear conviction of a prophet.

By means of assiduous prayer, I will lead you to the most profound experiences. . . . How happy I should be if all the world were to follow this path!

Please try to realize, my dear children, that I have come to earth to teach you to obey out of love, to pray out of love, and not because you are forced to do so by the crosses that you bear (November 29, 1984)

Pray with all your heart. I am your Mother and I want to teach you something very important: how to love. Jesus was able to pray without ceasing because He had such a great thirst for God and a fathomless desire for the salvation of souls. So pray! Pray! Pray! Only in prayer will you understand my love and the love of the Lord for you.

Father Jozo Zovko, pastor of the parish at Medjugorje when the apparitions began, speaking here with the pastor of the parish church of Fatima (Portugal).

On Good Friday, April 1, 1983, Father Tomislav Vlašić wrote an angry letter protesting the critical attitude of many in high places regarding the visions and the visionaries. He mentioned the matter to no one. Jelena met him soon after with a message from the Madonna which stated, *Do not complain about anyone. If there are problems, you must keep your smile and pray. Work started by God cannot be halted by anyone* (April 4, 1983).

As he attended the visionaries during those first years, he became more and more convinced of the wonderful and serious plan that God had in mind for him with respect to the work he was doing with "His" young people. He found that he was more open to the Spirit, that he had grown in respect, fortitude and the spirit of reflection by taking to heart the extraordinary events occurring around him. Presently he devotes himself to the charismatic community of *"Kraljice Mira,"* which takes its spirit from the messages of the Queen of Peace.

Father Tomislav Vlašić.
He was sent to Medjugorje when the pastor, Father Jozo, was put in jail. "At the first announcement regarding the apparitions, I said: 'The Gospel is enough for me. I believe. I have no need of apparitions.' Then I saw how pharisaical that was; even now I realize how very far I am from God, because the road opens before me ever more and more. . . ."

Now that he has been freed from work with the community in Medjugorje, Mary has made Father Slavko Barbarić her herald, her travelling prophet.

He has been invited to numerous towns and groups throughout Europe to proclaim the Madonna's urgent request for people to reform their lives, to return to a life of earnest prayer, the reception of the Sacrament of Reconciliation and the practice of fasting.

Recently he toured Brazil using every conceivable mode of transportation taking Mary's message to the remotest regions of that vast land in an attempt to light the Marian fire and awaken in many a deep desire for God.

Everywhere he goes, he says that one cannot deny the facts behind the Marian movement which started with the apparitions experienced by the visionaries of Medjugorje. Nor can it be stopped. Whenever he speaks of the events which have been occurring there, he does so from the personal experience he had while in the process of investigating them. To this day, he continues to monitor events there with an alert and open mind.

Father Slavko Barbarić.
Having succeeded Father Tomislav as the one in charge of the pilgrims who were coming to Medjugorje, he made a rigorously scientific study of the psychology of the group which formed around Mary. His conclusion was that "Medjugorje does not depend on the visionaries nor on the priests who work here."

"I am your gentle and loving mother"

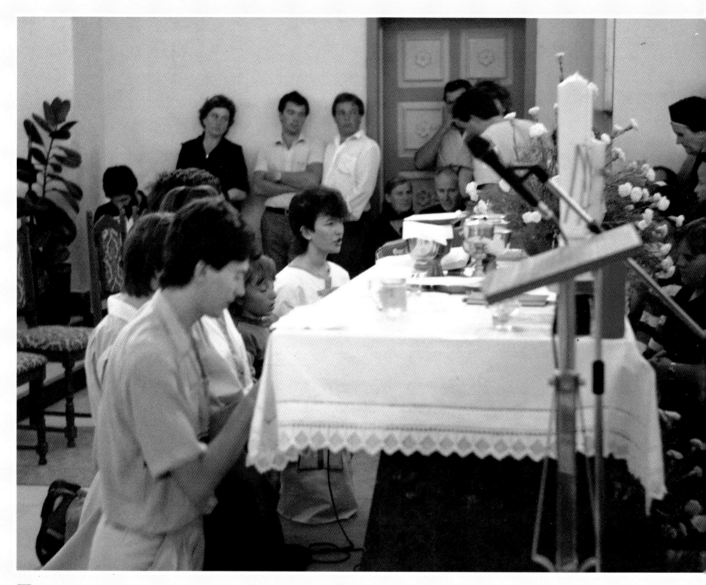

Turn over your hearts like you turn over the soil of your fields. . . . Don't desire to move about in these days in which the Holy Spirit is working in such a powerful way. . . . Your hearts are taken up with the things of earth and these preoccupy you. . . . Turn your hearts to prayer and ask the Holy Spirit to pour his graces out upon you!

Through Baptism Christians become "a chosen race, a holy nation, a royal priesthood, a people set apart" to worship God in Spirit and in truth. But Mary knows that their devotion often does not go very deep. And so she has dictated several prayers to remind Christians of their duty. With their help and her intercession, we can use them to seek the grace we need from God to practice true devotion.

Prayer of Devotion to the Sacred Heart of Jesus

O Jesus,
we know that you are kind
and that you gave Your Heart for us.
It is crowned with the crown of thorns
and with our sins.

We know that even today You pray for us
that we will not be led into temptation.
Stand by us, Jesus, so we will not fall and sin.
Through Your Sacred Heart grant us
the grace to always love each other.

There must be no more hatred among us.
Show us your love!
We all love You and want You,
with Your Shepherd's Heart,
to protect us from all sin.

Enter every heart, O Jesus!
Knock at their closed doors.
Be patient and untiring with us.
We have not yet
properly understood Your Will
and thus remain closed to You.

Knock steadfastly and grant us the grace
to open our hearts to You,
at least when we remember
the suffering You endured for us. Amen.

Prayer of Devotion to the Immaculate Heart of Mary

O purest heart of Mary,
filled with overflowing kindness,
show us your love.
Let the flame of your heart
descend upon all peoples.
Impress your love in our hearts
so that we shall long for you.

Our love for you is everlasting.
O Mary, gentle and humble of heart,
Stand by us when we sin.
You know that we are sinners
but grant that, through your
pure and maternal heart,
we shall all be healed
of everything that makes our souls sick.

Grant that we shall ever see
the goodness of your mother's heart,
and that we may be converted
through the flame of love it bears. Amen.
(to Jelena, November, 1983)

Up until April of 1985 the visionaries were the ones who, after the apparitions, led the praying of the Creed followed by the seven Our Fathers, Hail Marys and Glory Be to Gods in the church. Now one of the friars takes care of this.

The following prayer was given by the Madonna to Jelena so that the prayer group, founded at Mary's request, could recite it together:

A Fervent Request

O God, our heart is in profoundest darkness; and yet it is bound to Your Heart. Our heart is divided — one part belongs to You, the other to the devil. Let this not be so! Whenever our heart is divided, and one part desires the good while the other desires evil, let it be imbued with Your Light and become whole again.

Let not two different affections reign within us; two beliefs should never exist side by side: lies and sincerity, love and hate, truth and dishonesty, humility and pride should never live united within us. No! Help us lift our heart to You like the heart of a child; grant that peace occupy and delight our heart and never let our heart stop longing for it. Grant that Your Holy Will and Your Love find a dwelling place within us, so that we at least sometimes truly desire to be Your children. And in those moments, Lord, when we do not desire to be Your children, remember our past wishes, and help us to receive You anew again.

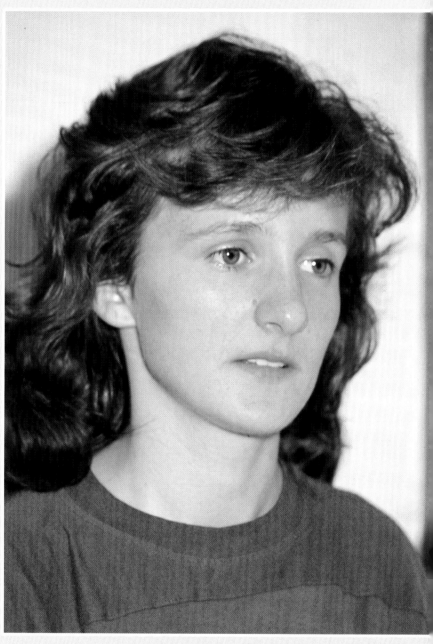

In this photo one can see Marijana Vasilj's gentle glance. She was born on October 5, 1971. Like Jelena, she was born in Medjugorje. Her father works in Germany and her mother often visits him. She has four brothers and sisters. Marijana attends nursing school. She has experienced an "Inner Voice" since Good Friday, 1983.

We open our hearts to You, so that Your Sacred Love can live within them; we open our souls to You, so they can be touched by Your Holy Mercy, which will help us see all our sins clearly, and will make us understand that what makes us unclean is called sin!

Lord, we wish to be Your children, humble and devoted, until we have become serious and good children, until we have become all that our Father desires.

Help us, Jesus our brother, to attain the forgiveness of our Father. And help us to be good to Him.

Help us, Jesus, to correctly understand what God grants us, because sometimes we refuse to do a good deed, believing it to be evil. We ask these things in Your Most Holy Name. Amen.

One day Jelena asked the Madonna, "Why are you so beautiful?" And Mary replied, *Because I love. If you want to be beautiful like me, you must love. But love is a grace of the Lord. It is a gift of the Holy Spirit. It cannot be bought nor can it be given away. All those who open themselves to God can have it.*

Jelena Vasilj: She was born on May 14, 1972 in Medjugorje. Her father is a farmer and has a large family. Jelena also attends nursing school. In contrast to the other visionaries, she has experienced an "Inner Voice" since December 15, 1982.

45

Those Whom Mary Chose

The boys and girls chosen by Our Lady have taken part in an exceptional spiritual itinerary. We see them here at the time when the visions began. The smallest, Jakov, was only ten; Vicka was seventeen. Today they have changed a lot, both physically and spiritually. Their prayers have attained an intensity that affects everyone. But the most astonishing thing about them is the warmth with which they receive pilgrims who besiege them to such an extent that they hardly have any time for themselves. That is not all. What strikes one most is the readiness of these young people to make extraordinary sacrifices and their readiness to do penance for others.

I will leave a sign for nonbelievers, before which many will come to believe. Not all, however, will reform their lives. . . . These, too, are my children and I suffer much for them, because they do not know what awaits them if they do not reform their lives and turn again to God.

The group of visionaries, formed on June 25, 1981, on the second day of their meetings with the Blessed Virgin. They include (from left to right): Mirjana, Vicka, Ivanka, Ivan, Marija, and in front of them all, little Jakov.

The Sign and the Secrets

From the very first days of the apparitions, the young people asked Mary to reveal herself to everyone, or to give some sign so that others would believe them because they were accused of being charlatans and of having invented everything. So Our Lady promised that she will cause a sign to appear on Mount Podbrdo. She has revealed the date to the visionaries and shown them what the sign would be like. They say that it is something tangible, stable and indestructible.

Mirjana was more specific: First there will be two warnings, then the sign will appear. If people do not reform their lives, a chastisement will follow. She recommends that all reform their lives at once: *When the sign appears, it will be too late for many.*

The sign will come, the Virgin assured them. *Don't worry. the only thing I want to insist on is this: be converted! Tell this to all my children right away. No worry and no suffering is too much for me to save you. I will ask my Son not to punish the world, but I beg you: be converted. You cannot imagine what will happen otherwise or what the Heavenly Father will send upon the earth. Therefore, be converted! Renounce everything; do penance. Thank all my children who have prayed and fasted. I will ask my Divine Son to be merciful when He passes judgment on the sins of mankind. I thank those who have accepted my call and have prayed. Continue to help me convert the world* (June 24, 1983).

Mary also promised to entrust each of the visionaries with ten secrets. As far as we know, they are not the same secrets for all six, since some seem to be of a personal nature. For the most part, though, they concern the future of the world.

Why, one wonders, at Medjugorje as at La Salette and at Fatima, are secrets concerning the future announced without being divulged? The Bible seems to give us a clue: the matters dealt with are not inevitable (one thinks of the preaching of Jonah about the destruction of Nineveh), but can be altered or attenuated through conversion and prayer. It seems that they also serve another objective: namely to maintain our striving for salvation, and to direct our gaze toward the Day of Judgment.

"You are a chosen people!"

The Queen of Peace has expressed her desire to make the parish of Medjugorje into a center from which her light will radiate.

My dear children, I have very specifically chosen this community, and I would like to guide it. I will watch over it with love, and would like all of you to belong to me. I thank you for responding to my call this evening. I would like you to gather around me and my Son in ever greater numbers. I shall give you a message every Thursday (March 1, 1984).

This evening I invite you in a very special way to revere — during this period of fasting — the wounds of my Son, which He received because of the sins of this parish. Join me in my prayers for the parish so that His suffering will become bearable. Thank you for responding to my call. Try to come in ever greater numbers! (March 22, 1984).

My children! This evening I especially ask you to worship the heart of my Son, Jesus. Make amends for the wounds inflicted on my Son's heart! His heart has been pierced by all manner of sin. . . . If your faith is strong, Satan is powerless. Follow the path of the messages. Reform your lives and be converted! (April 5, 1984).

My dear children! At this time I invite you to total devotion to God. Pray that Satan not sway you to and fro like branches in the wind. Be strong in the Lord. I would like the whole world to discover the God of Joy through you. Bear witness to the joy of God through your lives. God will help you and show you the way. I would like you to love everyone, good and bad, with my love. Only in this way shall love begin to rule the world. Children, you are mine! I love you and would like you to place yourselves totally in my hands so that I can lead you to God. Never stop praying and Satan will not be able to exploit you. Rather he will realize that you belong to me! I bless you with the blessing of peace! (May 25, 1988).

My dear children! At this time Satan is trying to thwart my plans; pray that he will not succeed. I will ask my Son, Jesus, to grant you the grace to recognize Jesus' victory in Satan's temptations (July 12 1984).

Today I invite you to renew your hearts. Open yourselves to God and hand over to Him all your troubles and the crosses which you bear so that God can turn everything into joy. Children, you cannot open yourselves to God if you do not pray. So from this day on, decide to set aside a certain time of day to meet God in peace and quiet. Thus, with God, you will be able to testify to my presence. I do not want to force you into anything, but give your time voluntarily to God, as his beloved children (July 25, 1989).

I invite you to pray, so that you can meet God in prayer. God is offering Himself to you. He gives Himself to you. But He wishes from you that you voluntarily answer His call. So dear children, set aside a certain time of day when you can pray in peace and humility, and can meet God, your Creator (November 25, 1988).

Prayer always leaves one in peace and serenity. My wish is that everyone might keep an image of the Sacred Heart in their homes and recite the Rosary in its entirety. Those who abandon themselves entirely into the hands of God no longer have any room in their hearts for fear.

"If you are weary . . . pray . . . and you will find rest"

Mary is a mother who understands our troubles. She knows that prayer is a wonderful, triumphant force.

I want you, dear children, to listen to my messages and to live by them! Every family should pray and read the Bible together. . . . I summon you to renew yourselves in prayer.

The devil is trying to thwart my plans with his cunning. He is trying to discourage you. . . . He has a great deal of influence in the world. . . . So pray more . . . pray with love. Be careful. . . . I have stayed with you for a long time to help you through this test. . . . Pray to the Holy Spirit that you might succeed in conveying my messages as they are given to you.

Once more I ask you to open your hearts to God, as spring flowers open to the sun. . . .

My dear children, I invite you to open yourselves to God. Have you seen, my children, how nature opens itself and gives life to the fruit of the field? Thus do I also invite you to a life with God and to total dedication to Him. My dear children, I am with you, and will always lead you into the true joy of life. I want each of you to discover the joy and love that can only be found in God, and that only He can grant. God desires nothing more from you than your devotion. Therefore choose God seriously, because everything else is transient! God alone is everlasting. Pray for the grace to discover the greatness and to appreciate the joy of life that God has bestowed on you! (May 25, 1989).

My children! I invite you to live the following words: I love God! Love of God is not widespread in the world. So pray!

I have nothing else to tell you: Pray! Pray! Pray! Go to your homes and pray before the crucifix. I am with you even in the smallest trials. . . . I need your prayers. . . . Help me!

My dear children, today I again invite you to completely reform your lives. This is difficult for those who have not chosen God. God, though, can give you anything you ask Him for. But you only turn to God when sickness, problems and difficulties prompt you to do so. Then you believe that God is far from you, that He does not hear you, and does not listen to your prayers. No, dear children, that is not true. If you are far from God, you cannot receive His grace because you do not ask for it in steadfast faith. I pray for you every day, and would like to lead you ever closer to God. But I cannot do so if you do not want it. Therefore, dear children, place your lives in God's hands. I bless you . . . (January 25, 1988).

The apparitions first took place on Mount Podbrdo, then in the chapel of apparitions, later in the parish house, and now by the church choir.

"Love drives away all fear"

I recommend group participation at prayer, especially to the young who are freer and can give themselves to prayer up to three hours a day.

1. Renounce all disordered passions.

2. Abandon yourselves totally to God.

3. Get rid of all fear once and for all.

I will lead your group for four years and will purify it. . . . The sole means for purifying one's heart is prayer . . . right up until you reach the moment in which you are totally present to God.

When you sin, it is as if you had fainted or lost consciousness . . . and your fears keep you far from me and you think of me as being very severe, or as someone very distant to you.

Pray! And I will pray with you!

Vicka during an apparition at her own home.

52

The ever-smiling face of Vicka.

You don't realize how great the mercy of God is towards you! . . . Thank Him for having allowed me to remain for such a long time in your midst.

Now I invite you to love; love in the first place your own families and then you will be able to accept with love all those who will come here. . . .

Dear children, open your hearts to the Lord of all hearts. Reveal to me all your sentiments and all your problems. I want to console you in your temptations. I want to fill you with peace, with joy, and with the love of God. If you knew how much I loved you, you would weep for joy.

53

My angels! Today I invite you to follow the path of holiness. Pray that you learn to appreciate the beauty and greatness of this path on which God reveals Himself to you in such a special way. Pray to be open to everything that God is doing through you. And pray for the grace to thank God for everything in your lives, and to rejoice in all that He does through each individual. I bless you (January 25, 1989).

Dear little ones, today I wish to tell you that God wants to test you; you will come through it well if you pray. God tests you through the very things which happen to you each day. So pray now that you may pass the test. With the grace that God gives you, you must open yourselves ever more to the Lord. Seek to grow closer to God with love. I thank you for having responded to my call (August 22, 1985).

The six young visionaries, whom the Virgin calls "My Angels," sing and pray during a religious function in the first year of the apparitions.

"You ask for many things. Ask for the Holy Spirit..."

Pilgrims listening to information regarding the events which are said to have been transpiring at Medjugorje.

The Spirit of God will suggest what you must say! (Jn 14:26)

Mary, the one who experienced the power of the Holy Spirit in a wholly unique way, very clearly points out to her children that it is impossible to live up to God's expectations without receiving the power of His gifts of inspiration and grace.

Pray that the Holy Spirit might enlighten you so that you can understand. . . . You ask for many things. Ask rather for the Holy Spirit; when He comes, all the rest will be given you besides.

Our task is to accept God's peace, to live it and to spread it, not with words only but with our lives.

Christians are mistaken when, looking to the future, they think of war and of evil. For a Christian, there is only one stance to take with regard to the future: it is that of hope in salvation.

My dear children! Tomorrow evening pray for the spirit of truth — particularly you who are from the parish — because you need the spirit of truth so that you can transmit my messages, just as I have given them to you, without adding or taking anything away. Ask the Holy Spirit to fill you with the spirit of prayer, so that you pray more. I, your mother, am telling you that you pray too little (June 9, 1984).

My children! At this time I especially invite you to open your hearts to the Holy Spirit! At this time, in particular, the Holy Spirit is working through you. Open your hearts and give your lives to Jesus, so he can work through your hearts and strengthen your faith (May 23, 1985).

From every part of the world people flock to Medjugorje. Here we see a Chinese priest in prayer.

"The dawning of a new era for the Church"

The church on the occasion of the anniversary of the
apparitions no longer holds the pilgrims who pour out
of the church and beyond the parish house.

Medjugorje, blossom of the Church's renewed youth.

"*I would like to lead this community*"

My dear children! You still do not fully comprehend the messages that God is sending through me. He grants you great mercies, but you do not understand. Pray to the Holy Spirit for inspiration! If you knew what great mercies God is granting you, you would pray unceasingly (November 8, 1984).

My dear children! At this moment you are experiencing the joy of God on account of the renewal of your parish. The devil is working even harder to take this joy from each of you. Through prayer you can totally disarm him and ensure your happiness (January 24, 1985).

My children! You have all experienced light and darkness in your lives. God lets all people experience good and evil. I invite you to carry the light for all those who are in darkness. Day in, day out, people who live in darkness come to your homes. Dear children, give them the light they seek! (March 14, 1985).

Dear children, I love you, and I have chosen this parish in a special way. Accept me and listen to my messages. Receive and live them so that you can profit by my presence in your midst (March 21, 1985).

My dear children! Thank you for starting to think about the glory of God in your hearts. This is the day when I had intended to give you no more messages because individuals have not accepted me. Still the parish has begun to be converted. Therefore I intend to give you messages such as have never been given anywhere since the beginning of the world (April 4, 1985).

My dear children! At this time I invite you above all to open your hearts to the Holy Spirit! In these days, in particular, the Holy Spirit is working through you. Open your hearts and give your lives to Jesus, because He is working through your hearts and is strengthening you in your faith (May 23, 1985).

My dear children! Again I invite you to pray with your hearts. Prayer should be daily sustenance to you, especially when you are so exhausted from working in the fields that you feel you cannot pray with your hearts. Pray anyway and you will overcome your exhaustion. Prayer will be a joy and a source of relaxation for you (May 30, 1985).

Pilgrims at prayer in Medjugorje. More than eight million pilgrims from all corners of the earth have already visited this little village, including bishops, famous theologians, crowds of priests, and people from every possible class and culture.

61

"Give yourselves unconditionally to God!"

On May 25, 1983, after a prayer group had been founded, the Madonna expressed her wish in the following words to Jelena: *Gather about you twenty or so young people who are willing to follow Jesus unconditionally. Get them together within a month. I will introduce them to the spiritual life. You can have more than twenty if you like. Adults and children are welcome, too, if they keep to the rules. I will expect these people to do penance, so that some beliefs shall be fulfilled. They will pray and fast for the bishop. They will give up those things they like most: for some it will be drinking, coffee, television or other pleasures. It is essential that there be those who are prepared to devote themselves to religious life. Others must be prepared to give themselves completely to prayer and fasting. I will tell them the rules by which they must live.*

Here are the rules that the Madonna dictated to Jelena on June 16:

1. *Renounce all passionate and evil desires. Avoid television and above all disgraceful broadcasts. Do not engage in excessive sports, immoderate eating and drinking, as well as alcohol, tobacco, etc.*

2. *Give yourselves unconditionally to God.*

3. *Banish from your heart forever every form of anxiety. Those who give themselves to God have no room for fear in their heart. There will still be difficulties, but they will serve to help you grow spiritually and to glorify God.*

4. *Love your enemies from your heart. Get rid of all hatred, bitterness, rash judgments and prejudice. Pray for your enemies and ask that God's blessings might descend upon you.*

5. *Fast on bread and water twice a week. Meet at least once a week as a group.*

6. *Every day you should devote at least three hours to prayer; of this, at least half an hour should be in the morning and half an hour in the evening; Holy Mass and the Rosary are included in these three hours. During the day try to find some free moments for prayer and receive Holy Communion as often as possible. Concentrate hard when you pray. Do not constantly glance at your watch while you are praying, but let yourselves be guided by the grace of God. Do not worry too much about worldly things; rather confide everything to your Heavenly Father in prayer. Those who worry too much cannot pray well because they lack the necessary inner peace. God will help to bring your earthly concerns to a good conclusion if you try to open yourself to His will.*

Those who go to work or school should set aside a half hour for prayer in the morning and the evening, and if possible also participate in the Eucharist. It is important that you let a spirit of prayer pervade your daily life; this means that the work you do should be accompanied by prayer.

7. Be cautious, for the devil tempts especially those who have decided to dedicate themselves wholly to God. He will try to persuade you that you pray too much and fast too much, that you should be like other young people who strive for pleasures. You must neither listen nor obey. Listen rather to my voice. And once your faith has been strengthened, the devil will not be able to harm you any more.

8. Pray often for the bishop and for those who bear responsibility within the Church. At least half of the prayer and sacrifices you make should be dedicated to this purpose.

I would like your group to be as beautiful as a flower in springtime. The love I have for you is very great, yet at times you refuse it and thus its effectiveness is diminished. Always be prompt to accept the gifts I offer you so that you may really profit from them.

Awake, O sleeper, arise
from the dead, and Christ
will give you light
(Ep 5:14).

"Pray for all the sick. Believe with steadfast faith!"

Mary's heart is like the heart of Jesus. Every human need triggers profound heartfelt compassion in her Son's heart and in her own, and both feel a deep desire to alleviate the suffering of those who are in distress.

Regarding those who are ill, Mary says, *Pray for all the sick. Be steadfast in your faith. I will help them as much as I can. I will ask my Son to come to their aid. But the most important thing is to be steadfast in faith. Many of those who are sick believe that it is enough to make a pilgrimage to this place and they will be instantly healed. Some of them do not even truly believe in God, and even fewer in the visions, yet they still expect 'the Gospa'* [a title by which the Madonna is familiarly addressed in Medjugorje] *to help them* (February 9, 1982).

At another time she said, *Be steadfast in your faith. Pray and fast. Be patient and pray to be healed* (November 26, 1981).

In answer to the question: "What can one do so that more people are healed?" Mary told the visionaries: *Pray! Pray and be steadfast in your faith. Recite the prayers that I have already asked you to say: seven Our Fathers, Hail Marys, Glory Be to Gods, and the Creed. Do more penance* (April 22, 1982).

In order to heal the sick, it is very important to say the following prayers: the Creed, seven Our Fathers, Hail Marys and Glory Be to Gods. It is important to fast on bread and water. It is good to hold your hands over the head of the sick person and to pray. It is good to anoint the sick person with Holy Oil [the oil used by the Church in the Anointing of the Sick]. *Not all priests have the gift of healing. In order to awaken this gift in himself, the priest must pray constantly and his faith must be strengthened* (July 25, 1982).

You must believe and pray; I cannot help anyone who does not sacrifice himself. The sick as well as those who are healthy must pray and fast for those who are ill. The stronger your faith and the more you pray and fast for this purpose, the greater will be God's grace and compassion (August 18, 1982).

A Prayer for the Sick

(to Jelena, June 22, 1985)

O my Lord,
This sick person present here before You
Has come to ask for something,
something that he (she) dearly longs for,
something that he (she)
considers to be very important.
Please, my Lord,
Grant that these words
enter his (her) heart:
"The important thing is to be spiritually sound!"

Protect him (her)
and alleviate his (her) suffering.
Your will be done in him (her).
May it rule over him (her) in everything!
If it be Your will that he (she) be well,
Grant him (her) health!
If it not be Your will that he (she) be well,
Help him (her) to bear the cross with courage.

I beg You, too, for us who are praying for him (her).
Cleanse our hearts so that we might be made
ever more worthy channels of Your grace.
I ask these things in Your most holy name. Amen.

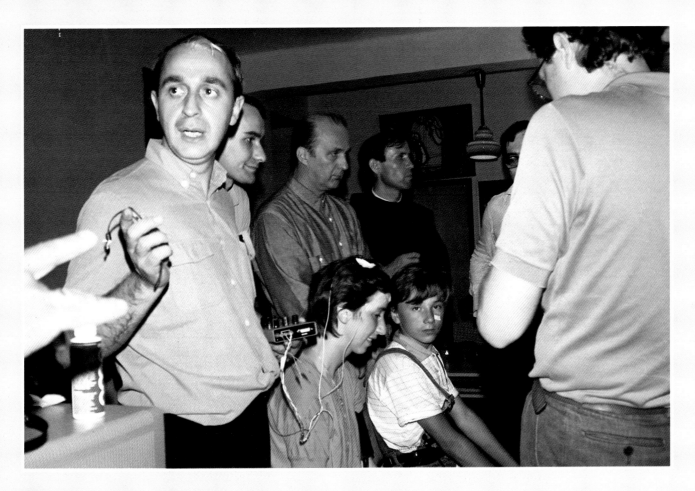

Doctor Frigerio (in the foreground facing) and a team of Italian doctors examine Marija and Jakov (September 8, 1985).

Making use of extremely sophisticated equipment, several teams of doctors, among them a French one under the direction of Doctor Joyeux and an Italian one under the direction of Doctor Frigerio, carefully examined the visionaries during the apparitions. Their conclusions exclude any form of fakery or hallucination as a possible explanation.

"Thank you for responding to my call"

Medjugorje is everywhere where there is an open heart. Mary makes this clear through the words with which she ends each message: "Thank you for responding to my call."

She continues: "I would like this village to become a source of grace for everyone.... I am close to all.... Live honestly and sincerely, in humility and love. This path will lead to me."

In her message of October 25, 1989 Mary begs all of us to
"Pray constantly, pray with your hearts. . . ."

Special Characteristics of the Messages

In all apparitions there are certain special characteristics. Naturally these do nothing more than emphasize one aspect or another of Revelation inasmuch as Christ is "the Mediator and at the same time the fullness of all Revelation," and "we now await no new further public revelation before the glorious manifestation of our Lord Jesus Christ" (*Dei Verbum*, 2 and 4).

The Medjugorje messages of the Blessed Virgin are very brief if they are taken one by one. They are more numerous than usual, however. Studying them, it at once becomes apparent that all of the points emphasized are to be found in Sacred Scripture. Here, though, they take on an accent not found in other apparitions. Their principal characteristics are:

1. The appeal for peace is constantly repeated. The woman of the vision even calls herself *"The Queen of Peace."* All the messages seem to be centered around this theme of peace: a return to God, a sincere conversion, prayer, fasting, etc. The theme of peace constitutes in the eyes of most what is the essential in these apparitions.

2. *God exists. In him everything has life. The one who finds God finds life.* The existence of God is the fundamental presupposition of religion; other apparitions have never insisted on this point. But it has become urgent for our day and age, marked as it is by widespread atheism. This is one of the main characteristics of Medjugorje, as is Mary's insistence on the praying of the Creed, a synthesis of the truths of the Christian faith. *My dear children, I invite you to devote yourselves totally to God. Everything you own should be in God's hands, because only in this way will you have joy in your hearts. My little angels, rejoice in everything you have. Thank God, because everything is a gift from God to you. This way you will give thanks for everything in your lives, and see God in everything, even in the smallest blossom. You will know great joy. You will know God* (April 25, 1989).

3. *Prayer, fasting, sacraments.* These have been the constant appeals of the latest apparitions approved by the Church: La Salette, Lourdes, Fatima. Here, though, there is something new: examples are furnished and precise details given. *Pray more and nourish your spiritual life through prayer. Grow spiritually and don't forget that this spiritual growth must continue your whole life long* (March 27, 1989).

Prayer. As a minimum the daily recitation of seven Our Fathers, Hail Marys, Glory Be to Gods and one Creed is advised; but a half-hour of prayer morning and evening is also recommended. A more prolonged prayer, up to three hours a day, is proposed for those who are able. The Rosary is important: *Call people back to praying the Rosary. I say to all priests, "Pray the Rosary. Dedicate time to its recitation."*

Fasting. A bread and water fast on Fridays is suggested; those who are more generous should fast on other days as well.

70

Mass and the Sacraments: assistance at daily Mass is encouraged. Regarding the Sacrament of Reconciliation: *If Christians were to go to confession once a month, soon whole regions would be healed spiritually.*

4. Further Gospel truths are also pointed out with some insistence: the existence of *heaven, hell, purgatory,* the *angels* and *Satan.* Much emphasis is placed on the Christian commandment of *charity,* especially the most difficult and heroic part of its practice, namely love for one's enemies. Here Mary's appeal for universal brotherhood must be stressed. She, in fact, presents herself as the *Mother of all,* just as God is the *Father of all.* Nor can one help but see in this teaching a confirmation of the ecumenical spirit of the Second Vatican Council, especially when one considers that this invitation is made in Yugoslavia where Catholics, Orthodox, Muslims, and atheists live side by side. All these teachings conform to the Gospels and to the practice of the Church. No new devotion is suggested here, nor is any new practice introduced.

Conclusion

Estimates now (1990) are that close to ten million pilgrims have paid a visit to Medjugorje since the visions first began nearly ten years ago. None of them went home disappointed. Indeed, many of them have but one desire, and that is to return. We have tried, in the pages of this album, to bring you a portfolio of images and messages which linger in the memories of those who have visited there. We know that many Christians who have not been able to go to Medjugorje have experienced the fascination of these visions and have formed prayer groups inspired by the messages reported in them. There have been moving stories about conversions which have taken place as a result of these events, many of them dealing with people who have never visited Medjugorje but have simply heard about the apparitions of "The Queen of Peace." This is Mary's hour. It is the time for man to sincerely turn back to God.

Some would prefer to wait for the ecclesiastical authorities to speak out and this is good. As many of our readers know, the first Commission to study these events was dissolved on May 2, 1986 and a new Commission appointed. It will take time before their conclusions are made public. Meanwhile it can be said that the content of the messages is basically evangelical, and the Gospel message doesn't require any further official declaration before being put into practice. That cannot wait. The parables of Jesus multiply warnings for those who beat about the bush or turn down the invitations of God, for example, the wedding guests who presented pretext after pretext in order to decline God's invitation to the feast, or the foolish handmaidens who arrived after the door had been closed, or the servant who buried his talent.

When Jesus came to earth, the angels sang, "Glory to God in the highest, and peace on earth to men of good will." The message of Medjugorje can be summed up as an appeal to render glory to God so that peace might indeed reign on earth. If one looks at the world closely, one cannot help but see that peace on earth is in peril in many places. One cannot ignore the fact that our scientific progress has forged an age of terrifying destructive potential; the disasters which would befall the human race in the case of a nuclear holocaust are unthinkable.

The Blessed Virgin did not come to Medjugorje, however, to predict catastrophes, but to teach us how to avoid them. At Fatima she predicted: *In the end, my Immaculate Heart will triumph.* At Medjugorje she has shown this, it seems, with a frequency which has no precedence in the history of the Church. The main message lies in her very presence, and only then in the invitation to follow her recommendations. At Lourdes, the Virgin appeared at the break of dawn; at Fatima, she appeared at noon. In Medjugorje, she appears as the sun begins to set. History's clock moves on inexorably. "Happy the servant whom the Master finds watching when He returns." The Mother of the Church is getting us ready to welcome Jesus, her Son.

Epilogue to the Second English Language Edition

If the authenticity of reported apparitions were to be judged by their spiritual fruits, there seems little doubt that the events which have been transpiring in Medjugorje have about them the ring of authenticity. The parish of Medjugorje has been transformed. Each evening there is a reconciliation service at the church with up to as many as thirty priests hearing confessions at one time. Most, if not all the families, have accepted Mary's call to fast on Fridays and to be faithful to the family recitation of the Rosary. Masses are crowded. Conversions are common. An atmosphere of forgiveness and peace reigns everywhere.

We know, however, that the Church very prudently reserves judgment in cases such as these because of the very real danger of mass hysteria and delusion. A new commission was appointed by the Yugoslavian National Conference of Bishops in May of 1986 to investigate the matter further after the original Commission was dissolved having failed to arrive at a definitive conclusion. As of this date no report has appeared with respect to the findings of the new Commission.

While awaiting an official declaration on the part of the Church, the publishers of the present volume have once again tried to present a moving description in word and picture of what many feel to be one of the most extraordinary religious occurrences of the decade. May this book contribute in some small way to the peace and salvation of the world.

Feast of the Assumption
August 15, 1990